Heinemann Library
n of Reed Elsevier Inc.
o, Illinois

mer Service 888-454-2279
ur website at www.heinemannraintree.com

signed by Joanna Hinton-Malivoire
oto research by Erica Martin
inted and bound in China by South China Printing Co. Ltd.

2 11 10 09 08
0 9 8 7 6 5 4 3 2 1

ISBN-10: 1-4034-9366-9 (hc)
ISBN-10: 1-4034-9370-7 (pb)

The Library of Congress has cataloged the first edition of this book as follows:

Mayer, Cassie.
  Canals / Cassie Mayer.
    p. cm. -- (Bodies of water)
  Includes bibliographical references and index.
  ISBN-13: 978-1-4034-9366-8 (hc)
  ISBN-13: 978-1-4034-9370-5 (pb)
  1. Canals--Juvenile literature. I. Title.
  HE526.M39 2007
  386'.4--dc22

3304   2006034048

Acknowledgements

The publishers would like to thank the following for permission to reproduce photographs: Alamy p. **17** (fstop2); Corbis pp.
4 (NASA), **5** (Free Agents Limited), **10** (Patrick Chauvel), **13** (Alan Schein Photography), **14** (Sergio Pitamitz), **23** (wide
canal: Sergio Pitamitz); FLPA p. **18** (Nigel Cattlin); Getty Images pp. **6** (Altrendo Travel), **7** (Hulton Archive), **19** (Photodisc
Green), **23** (field: Photodisc Green); Photolibrary pp. **8** (Hervé Gyssels), **9** (Jtb Photo), **11** (Walter Bibikow), **15** (Kindra
Clineff), **23** (narrow canal: Kindra Clineff); Robert Harding pp. **20** (Roy Rainford), **21** (Gavin Hellier); Waterways Photo
Library pp. **12** (Derek Pratt), **16** (Derek Pratt).

Cover photograph reproduced with permission of Getty Images/Digital Vision. Back cover photograph reproduced with
permission of Photolibrary (Kindra Clineff).

Every effort has been made to contact copyright holders of any material reproduced in this book. Any omissions will be rectified
in subsequent printings if notice is given to the publishers.

Bodies of Water

Canals

Cassie Mayer

Heinemann Library
Chicago, Illinois

© 2008
a divisi
Chicag

Custo
Visit

All r
me
wri

De
Ph
P

Contents

Canals 4

Types of Canals 12

What Canals Do 18

Canal Facts 22

Picture Glossary 23

Index 24

Canals

water

Most of the Earth is covered by water.

canal

Some of this water is in canals.

Canals look like rivers.

Canals are built by people.

Canals are waterways.

A waterway is like a road.

A waterway helps us reach places.

Canals go through land.

They connect two places by water.

Types of Canals

Canals connect rivers.

Canals connect lakes.

canal

Canals connect oceans.

Canals are wide.

Canals are narrow.

Canals go down hills.

Canals go through tunnels.

What Canals Do

Canals bring water to land.

The water is used to grow crops.

Canals help us move heavy things.

Canals help us move people.

Canal Facts

The Grand Canal is the oldest canal. It is in China.

The Grand Canal is also the longest canal.

Picture Glossary

 **crop** a plant that is grown for something such as food

 **narrow** short from side to side

 **wide** long from side to side

Index

crop, 19
hill, 16
lake, 12
ocean, 13
tunnel, 17

Note to Parents and Teachers
This title introduces canals and their uses. Discuss with children the similarities and differences between canals and other bodies of water, such as rivers. Use the primary source on page 7 to emphasize that canals are man-made bodies of water.

The text has been chosen with the advice of a literacy expert to enable beginning readers success in reading independently or with moderate support. An expert in the field of geography was consulted to ensure accurate content. You can support children's nonfiction literacy skills by helping them use the table of contents, headings, picture glossary, and index.